SOUTH EDINBURGH IN PICTURES

1. A time for celebration. Minto Street bedecked during the Coronation visit of Edward VII.

MORNINGSIDE ROAD LOOKING NORTH

2. A view up Morningside Road c. 1900. The toll house once stood on the right, now the busy post office area. No orderly queue for awaited cable car!

SOUTH EDINBURGH IN PICTURES

CHARLES J SMITH

ALBYN PRESS

First published 1989 by
Albyn Press Ltd
Whittingehame House
Haddington EH 41 4 QA
ISBN 0 284 98758 1

Also by Charles J Smith
and published by Albyn Press
Historic South Edinburgh, Vols. I—III

Printed in Yugoslavia by
Gorenjski Tisk Printing Company
Kranj

CONTENTS

ACKNOWLEDGEMENTS

In my introduction, I have acknowledged my gratitude to Mr Charles Skilton for publishing this collection of pictures of South Edinburgh and also to Mr Paul Harris for his assistance and advice. As will be evident below, my brother, William R. Smith, has contributed very many photographs and these have been indispensable. I am again greatly indebted to Mr Bill Weir, formerly photographer to Edinburgh University's Main Library, and his successor, Mr Malcolm Liddle, for the original processing of many of the illustrations. Mrs Maureen Smith very kindly typed the Introduction and captions. Many other people over the years, too numerous to mention, deserve my sincere appreciation.

For many illustrations I am indebted to the following: the late A. Hunter 1; Edinburgh City Libraries 7, 8, 55; C. P. Smith 9, 10, 11; Royal (Dick) Veterinary College 13, 14, 15, 16; the late Rev. E. Towill 17; courtesy of the Edinburgh Hebrew Congregation 21, 22; the late George E. Cramb 24, 25, 26; J. R. Webster 29, 30; The Yerbury Collection (available as post-cards) 32, 37, 44, 63, 88, 200; Longmore Hospital 40; the late Sir George Dick-Lauder 47, 48, 49, 50, 51, 52; Mrs J. B. Crossland 64; Rev. Logan Kirk 72, 73; Napier Polytechnic 82; Mr Duncan McAra 83; William R. Smith 85, 90, 91, 93, 101, 105, 107, 118, 127, 131, 133, 143, 144, 145, 151, 152, 155, 156, 163, 164, 165, 166, 182, 185, 189, 191, 199, 204, 209, 210, 211, 214, 226, 227, 234, 235, 241, 247, 251, 256, 263; Mr George Anderson 252, 255; Mr Gilmour Main 119, 132, 201, 203; Miss Jean Campbell 120; the Royal Commission on the Ancient and Historical Monuments of Scotland 123, 125, 147, 150; Mr Watson Kerr 129; Mrs J. Dunn 134; Miss C. M. Burt 138, 139; Mrs M. Forbes 141; Mr Brian Smith 160, 161; the late Miss E. Proudfoot 172; Rev. Dr R. Mathers 173; Mrs M. Meikle 179; Mr and Mrs R. A. C. Linzee-Gordon of Cluny and Dr J. C. B. Cooksey 194; Miss Janet Ratcliffe Barnett 206; Mrs Una Wallace 215; Royal Edinburgh Hospital 221, 222, 223, 224, 225; Rev. Sister Valerio 229, 233; Mrs A. Joe 230; South Morningside School 245; the late Mr W. A. Sharp 248, 258, 264; Mr Robin Hill 265, 270, 272; the late Mrs J. Slater 273; and the Scottish Tourist Board 279.

INTRODUCTION

Local history is now of considerable interest and in Edinburgh many books have appeared over the years stimulating this and responding to it with the fruits of much research. During the past decade, I have been grateful to Mr Charles Skilton for kindly publishing my four volumes on Historic South Edinburgh. The first two volumes presented a general history across many centuries of the development of a large area of the city, once the ancient Burgh Muir, southwards to Swanston. Volumes Three and Four contained biographies of a large number of famous, notable, eccentric and, I hope, at least interesting people who have resided in South Edinburgh, a great many of them during the 19th century, and mostly touched upon briefly in my earlier volumes. It seemed to me that they merited greater attention.

Mr Paul Harris in the introduction to his fascinating, highly successful and copiously illustrated "Edinburgh Since 1900" comments that, as every newspaper editor is aware, "a good picture is worth a thousand words". Certainly for very many people, this is a very important if not essential feature of books on local history: that they contain a substantial number of relevant illustrations. And indeed, again, for many people the above newspaper editor's edict being their own, they do not necessarily wish to have a great deal of text and minute historical detail, important and necessary as that may be in another context. In this book, such considerations have been kept in mind.

In my previous books, Mr Charles Skilton has published a substantial number and variety of illustrations, although for reasons of space and cost, many others had to be omitted. In the individual and courses of lectures on South Edinburgh which I have given over many years, I have shown a large collection of slides and transparencies, many of which I have been pleased to learn have proved of special interest to audiences and class members. Indeed, many people have suggested that the illustrations for my books and lectures, plus certain others necessarily omitted, might appear in a published collection. I am therefore very pleased that Mr Charles Skilton, my publisher, and Mr Paul Harris, such an experienced editor and selector, have all collaborated in producing this book.

Many excellent illustrated publications on the history of Edinburgh have had special themes viz., "The People of Edinburgh": at work, play etc., and now with the opening of "The Peoples' Story" in the former Canongate Tolbooth Museum, there will be increased interest in the city's social history. I would like to think, therefore, that these illustrations now published are not just an isolated, unrelated collection, but have their own special theme. This is the development of South Edinburgh, a very large part of the city, with its ancient associations, into a great and desirable residential area, which for several reasons could well be described as Edinburgh's "Other New Town".

A well-known, and indeed important, new and historic chapter in Edinburgh's development began when, the Old Town having become so overcrowded and confined within its ancient boundary and defensive walls, expansion had to take place. Many people, including Sir Walter Scott, thought that the city's "New Town" would arise to the South, to be built upon the for long remote and unexploited but nonetheless potentially attractive area of the ancient Burgh Muir, extending roughly from the old South and Burgh Loch, which became the Meadows, southwards to the Pow or Jordan Burn, then the city boundary, and westwards from Holyrood Park to Myreside and Craig-

lockhart. Of course, in fact, the city's worldfamous classical New Town was to arise in phases beyond the drained Nor' Loch, and the great exodus of people of means took place across the first North Bridge of 1772, the realised dream of Lord Provost George Drummond, into young architect James Craig's "windy parallelogram" of elegant squares and terraces of Hanovarian names, with Princes Street perhaps becoming best known.

Edinburgh's expansion northwards, however, did not stop a steady "mushroom" development to the south, its various districts originating from the feuing act of the Burgh Muir in 1585. In 1788 less than 20 years after the building of the first North Bridge, the South Bridge with its 19 arches spanning the deep gorge of the Cowgate, was completed. While prior to this important development, a certain number of fine houses had been built in George Square and adjacent Buccleuch Terrace, the new bridge greatly increased access to the south and before long systematic development began.

One origin suggested for the name Newington is "New Town Meadow" and, indeed, it was in this district that the first substantial "building programme" began. The feuing superiority of Newington was acquired in 1805 not by a property developer as such, but by one of Edinburgh's leading surgeons. of the time, Dr Benjamin Bell, a native of Dumfriesshire and something of a "financial wizard", who with the collaboration of another noted Edinburgh medic, Dr Alexander ("Lang Sandy") Wood, the young Walter Scott's one-time doctor, began the development of the Newington estate. Early plans show the quite rapid building of houses of high standard and the laying out of streets named after Dr Benjamin Bell's Dumfriesshire associations. Mayfield's development was to follow later. In 1805 Dr Bell built for himself, Newington House in Blacket Avenue, in the midst of his new, rapidly developing residential area. His own enjoyment of Newington House was short-lived, his death occurring there in 1806. His son continued the "Other New Town" planning. Minto Street became the important "New Road to the South". Newington attracted professional people and successful business men. At each end of Blacket Avenue and Mayfield Terrace, gates were built and closed nightly at 10.00 p.m. to preserve the select district's amenity.

Strictly, the drainage of the ancient South or Borough Loch over nearly two centuries and the creation and landscaping of that most pleasant open green space, the Meadows, is rather outwith the boundaries of South Edinburgh except that it led to much easier access to the Sciennes and Bruntsfield districts and the consequent development there of new residential areas. Sciennes, of 16th century origin with the convent there of St. Catherine of Sienna, had other early villas, most notable perhaps being Sciennes House where the only recorded meeting of Robert Burns and the then young Walter Scott took place in the winter of 1786—87. Local street names now commemorate the past in the midst of a district of fine terraced villas. The then new Royal Hospital for Sick Children, Sir George Washington Browne's creation of 1895, associated this ancient district with Edinburgh's renowned medical fame.

The very early road to the south, Causewayside, was straddled by ancient mansion houses such as the reputedly 16th century Wormwood Hall and, later, picturesque and often two-storey cottages in the late 18th century, the homes and work places of various weavers, dyers and other craftsmen. Grange Court originally had a community of such men and their families. The rural-like village of Summerhall gave way to the building of a new Royal (Dick) Veterinary College. Adjacent to Grange Court lived a number of Jewish families, originally immigrants, with a little cemetery entered from one-time Braid Place and early synygogues in other parts of the city. When, by the late 19th century, on account of a trade slump, many of Causewayside's craftsmen had gone, people moved in from run-down parts of the city and the district was described as "the worst part of Edinburgh". Here unemployment, poverty, heavy drinking and bad housing was rife. The lay missionary of the early Newington United Free Church in Duncan Street James Goodfellow did heroic work amidst such problems and many decimating infectious diseases. Wooden barricades between Minto Street and Causewayside prevented the reputed vandals of the latter entering the select Newington district.

After Newington, the other most attractive then still rural part of South Edinburgh drawing people out from the city and even from the classical New Town, was the Grange, with its origins in the 12th century Grange or farm lands of the monks of St. Giles who here first began to bring the rough, unpromising wasteland of the Burgh Muir under cultivation. The Dick and Lauder families, early owners of the Grange lands, and notably Sir Thomas Dick-Lauder, are today commemorated by local street names. Sir Thomas by his feuing plan of 1825 paved the way for the creation of a particularly pleasant sunward district of specially fine villas of attractive architecture, built in spacious and secluded streets.

Nowhere did Edinburgh's "other New Town" develop so steadily or with such density as in the Bruntsfield area, again with its origins in a great mansion house, the 16th century Bruntsfield House, the Edinburgh family seat of the Warrender family. Sir George Warrender, in his great feuing and building plan of 1876, gave rise to a quite unique network of streets and terraces, of varied architecture, for long world-famous as virtually a world of its own of students "digs". Yet space was still found for two large High Schools, Bruntsfield Hospital and a University Institute of Public Health. There was also a large, famous and quite ancient short-hole golf course, Bruntsfield Links, a green space protected by early Town Council legislation. Amidst so much late 19th century building, the ancient Bruntsfield House was preserved and skilfully restored while, matching it in age, the nearby, Whitehouse also, in part, still stands, visibly incorporated into what became part of St Margaret's Convent opened in 1835.

At the beginning of Bruntsfield Place at Barclay Church, the present day Wrights Houses, beside the Golf Tavern, recall the truly ancient reputedly 14th century mansion house, once known as Boroughmuir Castle, built in what became Gillespie Crescent commemorating James Gillespie, the wealthy Colinton snuff merchant whose generous legacy created a "hospital" for poor people and a school for needy boys, on the Wrychtishousis site, forerunner of the James Gillespie's High School of today.

In Greenhill, reached northwards up Bruntsfield Place, again an early mansion house gave way to a fine residential district, where, notably in Greenhill Gardens, houses of greatly varied architecture became the homes of people distinguished in many fields, attracted by the secluded surroundings. So, too, westwards from "Holy Corner" with its four churches of different denominations, Merchiston Tower had

been the early 16th century family seat of the illustrious Napier family, most notably of John Napier, world renowned mathematician.

Moving steeply up to Churchhill, street plaques recall that here was Boroughmuirhead, highest point on the ancient Burgh Muir, of magnificent vista over Edinburgh and to the south. Dr Thomas Chalmers, famous churchman of the 1843 Disruption had the first villa built for himself at No. 1 Churchhill in 1842. Eastwards, Morningside House in secluded Clinton Road was the district's first villa, built in 1726, and now surrounded by late 19th century castellated mansions typical of the district.

Opposite the Churchhill Theatre, opened by the city in 1965 in the vacated Morningside High Church, a short section of Morningside Road was originally named Waverley Terrace, and running southward from it was Marmion Terrace. Albert Terrace, once Doo Loan, anciently led to the long vanished weavers village of Tipperlinn around which the Royal Edinburgh Hospital arose.

Looking down from the brow of Churchhill on Morningside, one of Scotland's busiest suburbs, it is difficult to think that James Grant, a century ago, described Morningside village from here as "a group of trees, a row of cottages and a blacksmith's forge". Here, by the end of the 19th century had developed one of the most populous and attractive areas of the southern "New Town". Morningside's origins and growth had been quite different from these districts arising around an ancient mansion house or castle. They centred on a group of smiddies or blacksmith's shops, now long replaced by the Public Library and the Merlin. Here carters and farmers made their first stop after riding in from Biggar and the south, Lothianburn, Swanston and the other important farms nearby of Greenbank, Plewlands, Braid and Canaan, where originally around 1790 at Denholm's, then at Dick Wright's, horses were attended, carts repaired and other work done. From such agriculturally related origins, Morningside grew, with an inn, the Volunteers Rest (now "The Canny Man") as a carters rest. In 1823, the little schoolhouse was opened and, in 1838, Morningside Parish Church was completed. Morningside House (now site of "Scotmid") was the first "big house", Falcon Hall coming later. In portraying the early features of Morningside, old photographs kindly provided by many local people have been invaluable.

With the establishment of the Edinburgh Suburban Railway in 1884, a vast improvement on the cable cars and other early road transport, the old village, already growing steadily, virtually mushroomed overnight. The high tenements of Morningside Road were up by the turn of the century. At the same time "the tinkling chisels" (Stevenson's colourful words) created that other feature of Morningside which, Stevenson again, derisively named "villadom", encircling until it eventually replaced farmland and "endangered meads". When the Hermitage of Braid estate was sold, its 18th century owner Charles Gordon of Cluny in Aberdeenshire, was commemorated by the street names as also in Midmar and Corrennie. Happily the Hermitage of Braid remains through Mr John McDougal's generosity, now pleasant parkland for the citizens of Edinburgh and a unique Country Information Centre.

When the important and extensive Plewlands farm was sold in 1880 and the surrounding land feued out, notably in the plan of 1882, a whole new district was to arise, under the shadow of the 16th century mansion house of Old Craig and later the quite massive but impressive Craighouse Hospital of 1894 for mental disorders, more recently the Thomas Clouston clinic.

Also, as seen from Craighouse Hill, another two of Edinburgh's important "institutions" were built at Greenbank, the city Poorhouse and the City Fever Hospital. To the south-west under the shadow of wester Craiglockhart Hill, a hydropathic of short duration became the 1914—18 War Military hospital, where the famous war poets Siegfried Sassoon and Wilfred Owen were patients. The important Convent of the Sacred Heart, in the vacated hospital building, noted for its teacher training, was sold some years ago to Napier Polytechnic. Here, a very large pleasant residential district has grown up beside the old tower's ruined remains and two old mansion houses.

In the 1930's, with the almost phenomenal growth of classical bungalows and villas in the Greenbank area, the old farmland disappeared. Happily, in the beautifully, skilfully landscaped Braidburn Valley Park, a great deal of the attraction of this rural area has been preserved, even enhanced.

Robert Louis Stevenson, making his way on foot from the University through Morningside and Comiston to Swanston Cottage, would still today recognise many features of his day, despite the growth of the extensive residential districts of Fairmilehead, Caiystane, Oxgangs and, more recently, Hunters Tryst. For all of the changes, much of the atmosphere remains, as at Swanston itself, to enable us to appreciate the deep nostalgia for South Edinburgh and the Pentland Hills which the years in his South Seas home could never dispel.

The tropics vanish and seems that I,
from Halkersyde, from topmost Allermuir,
or steep Caerketton,
dreaming, gaze again.

THE MEADOWS

3. The ancient Borough or South Loch: source of water for brewers at today's Boroughloch end and for houses in area, and also an important bird sanctuary. Between 1722 and 1863 it was drained to become the Meadows. Prominent building was Merchant Maiden's Hospital, later to become Mary Erskine School. The vacated building was occupied by George Watson's College.

4. The drained Borough or South Loch gradually became the Meadows.

5. The Dutch style house, now No. 6 Hope Park Square, near Boroughloch area of the Meadows. Built by Sir Thomas Hope of Rankeillour in 1770. Hope began drainage of Boroughloch c. 1720.

6. Millerfield House, home of the Miller family. Built c. 1820. William Miller became an engraver of renown. Today's street off Melville Terrace commemorates the family.

7.8. The large pavilion of International Exhibition of Industry, Science and Art opened in West Meadows in 1886. Planned by Sir James Gowans.

9. The Prince Albert sundial in the West Meadows, a souvenir of the great International Exhibition of 1886. Prince Albert opened the event.

10. Two pillars were built at the west end of Melville Drive, comprising segments of stone from many qarries and with the coats of arms of the Scottish burghs. Erected by Master Builders and Operative Masons of Edinburgh during the Exhibition.

11. The Whale Jawbone Arch at the entrance to Jawbone Walk from Melville Drive. Presented to the city by the Zetland and Fair Isle Knitting Stand after the Exhibition.

12. The building of the then new Royal (Dick) Vetinary College at Summerhall, completed in 1916.

13. The College after completion. Causewayside begins on the right.

14. Houses at the pleasant and quite rural district of Summerhall, beside the Meadows, and demolished to make way for the Royal (Dick) Veterinary College in 1913.

15. William Dick, born 1793, son of a blacksmith in the Canongate's Whitehorse Close, who founded the first Veterinary College in Clyde Street in 1833. Transferred to the present site 1913. College bears his name.

16. Dick's first veterinary college in Clyde Street. Note stone figure of a horse (Dick's special interest) above the doorway which was transferred to new college's Summerhall Square side entrance.

17. A telling 1930s scene at the corner of Buccleuch Terrace at Hope Park. The soup kitchen was provided by Newington - St. Leonard's Church.

18. The north aspect (originally the front and entrance) of Sciennes Hill House, still standing behind No. 7 Sciennes House Place off Causewayside. Here took place the only known meeting of Robert Burns and young Walter Scott in the winter of 1786-87. It was then the home of Professor Adam Ferguson.

19. Jews Close, once in Causewayside near the entrance to Sciennes House Place. There was a small Jewish cemetery nearby, still to be seen on the south side of Sciennes House Place.

20. Old houses in Causewayside until relatively recently, with premises of now defunct Bertrams Engineering Works at rear. Replaced by modern flats.

21. An early Jewish Synagogue once in Graham Street, off Lauriston Place.

22. As the small Edinburgh Jewish Community developed there was a succession of Synagogues. This one was in Park Place.

23. A corner of Grange Court before restoration.

24. Girls pack biscuits by hand in Middlemass' factory.

25. Middlemass' large biscuit factory opened in Salisbury Place, South Side, in 1869. Demolished in recent years to provide the site for the Scottish Science Library and Map Department of the National Library.

26. The original premises of Middlemass, the noted Edinburgh biscuit manufacturer opened in 1853, at north corner of West Preston Street and South Clerk Street.

27. Grange Court, Causewayside, once the residence of weavers and craftsmen. Following their departure, the houses deteriorated over a long period. There was a skilled restoration of the Court in 1969.

28. Wormwood Hall, an ancient mansion house which once stood on the east side of Causewayside; reputedly built in 16th century.

29. Mr James Goodfellow, lay missionary of Newington United Presbyterian Church who laboured in Causewayside and outlying districts for nearly fifty years. Causewayside, for a period the worst bit of Edinburgh, presented great problems of unemployment, disease, poverty and drunkenness.

30. The original premises of Newington United Presbyterian Church in Duncan Street of the mid 19th century, which transferred to what became Salisbury Church at the corner of Grange Road and Causewayside in 1863.

DUNCAN STREET,
Opened 9th January 1848.

GRANGE ROAD,
Opened 15th November 1863.

31. Grange Loan at Causewayside, c. 1850.

32. Causewayside looking Southwards to Liberton, showing Grange Toll gates c. 1850.

33. Main entrance to the Royal Hospital for Sick Children, Sciennes Road, opened in 1895. The architect was Sir George Washington Browne.

NEWINGTON

34. South Bridge, completed 1788. Only one of the bridge's concealed 19 arches across deep Cowgate valley is visible, above this thoroughfare.

35. The North Bridge, opened 1772, permitted a great exodus of people of means from the overcrowded Old Town to the elegant and classical New Town across the drained Nor' Loch. South Bridge, built 16 years later, encouraged development to the South, notably to Newington.

36. South Bridge from the Cowgate.

37. Taxi: Well . . . pony and trap. Actually this photograph shows the Rails Parcel Service at Newington. The early "Red Star"!

38. Pillars at the west entrance to Blacket Avenue, off Minto Street and Dalkeith Road. Originally, gates were installed at each end, as also with Mayfield Terrace, and closed at 10 p. m. nightly to preserve the amenity of the new district.

39. Newington House, built in Blacket Avenue, off Minto Street by Dr. Benjamin Bell c. 1806. He died here a year later. Eventually it was acquired by the National Institution for the War Blinded. Demolished 1966.

40. A Royal Visit during the early days of the Longmore Hospital, Salisbury Place. Can anyone identify the occasion?

41. Newington Station on the Edinburgh Suburban Railway. Opened 1884. Closed 1962. A recently mooted possibility of reopening.

42. Mayfield Church, built by Hippolyte Blanc 1879, during the serious fire in 1969. Over £50,000 damage, but it was soon rebuilt.

43. Prestonfield House, Priestfield Road, built in 1689 to replace the earlier mansion destroyed by student demonstrators in 1681. It was the home of several generations of Dick family and is now a well known hotel.

44. Lady Road c. 1900. Now a rather busier street with the advent of the Cameron Toll Savacentre.

THE GRANGE

45. The original 12th century Grange of St. Giles — "Sanct Geilie's Grange" — a simple tower built by monks of St. Giles as a farmhouse in the then wasteland of the Burgh Muir. The site was in today's Grange Loan.

46. Grange House built on the site of the ancient tower by Sir Thomas Dick-Lauder 1827; architect W. H. Playfair. Mecca of Edinburgh's literary circle, artists and scholars.

47. Grange House: demolished 1936.

48. Grange House: the sitting room. Scene of 19th century Edinburgh literary gatherings.

49. Grange House: the dining room.

50. Entrance to Grange House in Grange Loan, midway between Lauder Road and Lovers' Loan.

51. After demolition of Grange House in 1936 the Lauder griffins (actually wyverns), once above gateway, were placed on pillars between Lovers Loan and Lauder Road in Grange Loan.

52. Entrance to Grange House: close up.

53. Old cottages at east end of Grange Loan 1865. Grange House on the right.

54. The Penny Well, once stood above the spring at the corner of Grange Loan and Findhorn Place. A penny a cupful of water! Long since covered-in.

WHITEHOUSE & BRUNTSFIELD

55. St. Margaret's Convent, Whitehouse Loan, established by Bishop Gillis 1835. Built around early 16th century White House the remains of which are still extant. Closed 1985. It became Gillis College, St. Andrews and Edinburgh RC Seminary in 1986.

56. 16th century Bruntsfield House, Whitehouse Loan, centuries-old family seat of the Warrender family. After vacation and serious deterioration, admirably restored as administrative centre of James Gillespies High School for Girls, now a co-educational High School.

57. The former Usher Institute of Public Health in Warrender Park Road. Opened 1902, it was the gift of Sir John Usher and Alexander Low Bruce (of William Younger's, Holyrood) resulting from Louis Pasteur's 1884 Edinburgh visit. It was vacated in 1986 and is now student flats.

58. Dr Sophia Jex-Blake

59. Bruntsfield Hospital for Women and Children, Whitehouse Loan, opened in 1911 at the rear of the foundress, Dr. Sophia Jex Blake's home (Bruntsfield Lodge) in Greenhill Park. Earlier "hospitals" in Dr. Sophia Jex Blake's house in Manor Place and then Grove Street. The hospital was closed amidst protests 1989.

60. Bruntsfield House becomes part of James Gillespies High School in 1966.

61. Early golf on Bruntsfield Links, first played here in the 15th century.

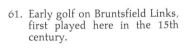

62. The ancient Golf Tavern, once known as "Golf Hotel".

63. "Putting Out". A tense moment. No caddy cars, matched sets, ... or the golfers' gear: Bruntsfield Links. c. 1886

64. Barclay Church, prominent Edinburgh landmark, built by Frederick Thomas Pilkington 1864 as the Free Church. His design was controversial with its 200 feet high ornamented steeple-towers dwarfing Glengyle Terrace and the nearby golfers.

65. The trophy still played for annually on Bruntsfield Links short hole course. Donated in 1959 by Mr Michael Shaw, for nearly 50 years "mine host" of Golf Tavern.

66. The reputedly 15th century "Golf Tavern" under the shadow of Barclay Church. For long the weary "gowfers'" welcome 19th Hole.

67. Your shopping delivered to your door. No trouble for Blanche, one-time "high class" Bruntsfield Place licensed grocer.

68. Wrychtishousis, an ancient mansion house once called Burgh Muir Castle was reputedly built in the 14th century, on the south side of the present Gillespie Crecent. It was demolished in 1800 and replaced by James Gillespie's Hospital

69. Gillespie's Hospital, replaced Wrychtishousis in 1802 from a generous legacy from wealthy Colinton snuff merchant, James Gillespie. Initially for elderly needy people, with "poor boys" school. It became a fee-paying school in 1887, moved to vacated Boroughmuir School on Bruntsfield Links in 1915 and Whitehouse Loan in 1966. Original hospital became Royal Blind Asylum workshops 1922; then sadly demolished in 1975.

GREENHILL

70. Greenhill House, original manor house of the district. Stone sculpted plaque by architect Sir George Washington Browne, at the corner of Bruntsfield Gardens and Place. The house was demolished in 1884.

71. Private burial ground, at No. 1 Chamberlain Road, of John Livingstone, early owner of Greenhill estate who died during the plague epidemic 1645. His son probably built Greenhill House.

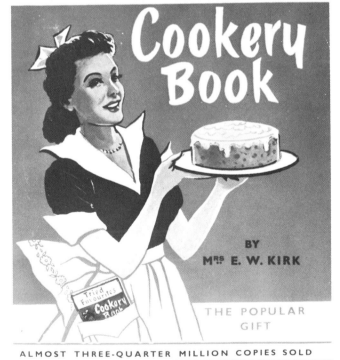

72. Hopefield Cottage, 17 Greenhill Gardens. One of a group of houses in the earlier north section (1850) of this pleasant street of varied architecture. Home of Mrs Eliza Kirk who here wrote her famous cookery book "Tried Favourites" (c. 1900).

73. Mrs Eliza Kirk with "Juno" who had been found abandoned.

74. Title page of "Tried Favourites".

75. The Pope with an ecumenical gathering from other churches in the private chapel at St Bennet's, Greenhill Gardens, 1982.

76. Pope John Paul II exchanges gifts with the Moderator of the Church of Scotland, Professor John McIntyre at "St. Bennets", Greenhill Gardens, the then residence of Cardinal Gordon Joseph Gray, during the Pontiff's visit to Scotland 1982.

638.

The Fountain, Morning

77. "Holy Corner", the junction of Morningside Road, Colinton Road and Chamberlain Road. Churches of four different denominations are to be found there. The fountain (left) served to water horses of the old horse-drawn trams.

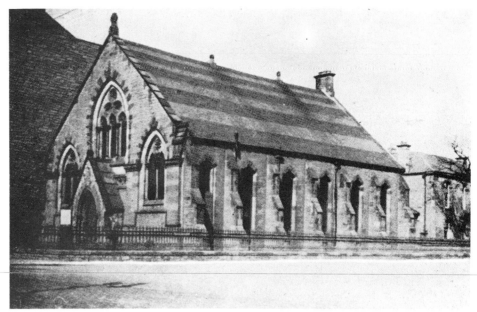

The Morningside Athenæum.

○

Poetic & Dramatic Recital

BY

MISSES WEBLING

(JOSEPHINE, ROSALIND, AND PEGGY)

On Tuesday, February 17, 1885, at 8 p.m.

PROGRAMME.

The Jackdaw of Rheims,	*Peggy.*	.	Ingoldsby
The Cloud,	*Josephine.*	.	Shelley
The Royal Princess,	*Rosalind.*	.	C. Rossetti
My Old Overcoat,	*Peggy.*	.	Turner
The Clown's Baby,	*Josephine.*	.	Anon
The Owl Critic,	*Rosalind.*	.	Anon
Ho-Ho of the Golden Belt,	*Peggy.*	.	J. G. Saxe
The Swineherd,	*Josephine.*	.	Hans Andersen
The Faithful Lovers,	*Rosalind.*	.	Anon

SELECTIONS FROM HENRY V. (SHAKESPEARE).

Act 3, Scene 4.   Act 5, Scene 2.

CHARACTERS.

Henry, King of England,	.	Josephine
Katherine, Princess of France,	.	Rosalind
Alice, Lady in Waiting,	.	Peggy

(In Costume.)

ADMISSION, ONE SHILLING.   Children, HALF-PRICE.
Members of the Athenæum, FREE.
Tickets and Programmes may be had at the Athenæum.

78. The original North Morningside Church building at the north-west corner of Chamberlain Road. When moved to the fine 12th century church opposite, vacated premises were opened by Mr George Seton of St. Bennets, Greenhill, as Morningside Atheneum, a club for literary and musical interests, with a library.

79. Programme of an evening at Morningside Atheneum.

80. The 16th century Merchiston Tower from 1608-17, home of world renowned mathematical genius, John Napier. There is an isolated outpost on remote Burgh Muir.

81. First named "Merchiston Castle" when school of this name established here in 1833, by Charles Chalmers. The school moved to Colinton Road in 1930.

82. After the removal of Merchiston Castle School, Merchiston Tower was used only sporadically. The fabric deteriorated. The tower, skilfully restored, eventually became the centrepiece of the then Napier Technical College, opened by distinguished scientist Sir Edward Appleton in 1964, at a cost of £2 million.

83. In Napier Road, a little down Colinton Road, the controversial but brilliant architect Sir James Gowans built this "astonishing house", "Rockville", in 1858 as his home. It incorporated 2-feet square stone modules from many quarries. It was also known as the "Sugar Loaf", "Pagoda House", and "Chinese House". Demolished 1966.

84. A well known figure in the Merchiston and Morningside districts was Theodore Napier of West Castle Road. An ardent Jacobite, he made an annual pilgrimage to Fotheringhay where Mary, Queen of Scots, was beheaded. He died in 1900.

CHURCHILL

85. The Churchhill Theatre, formerly Morningside High Church, built in Italianate style by Hippolyte Blanc in 1892 for Morningside Free Church. After re-union of this Church with Morningside Parish Church in 1960, the vacated building was opened as an excellent theatre by Edinburgh Corporation 1965, at cost of £67,000. An International Festival Centre.

87. Prize label of this private school, once at No. 92 Morningside Road c. 1850.

86. An early shop which succeeded O'Hagan c. 1920.

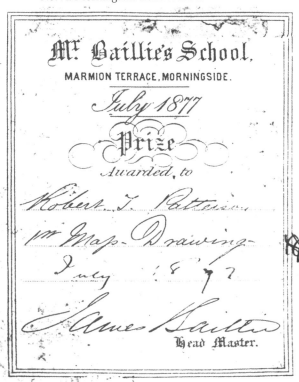

Mr Baillie's School,
MARMION TERRACE, MORNINGSIDE.

July 1877

Prize

Awarded to

Robert T Patterson

1st Map Drawing

July 1877

James Baillie
Head Master.

88. Shop formerly at No. 102 Morningside Road c. 1890. Note "Marmion Terrace" on left, the name of this section of Morningside Road prior to 1885.

89. Dr. Thomas Chalmers

90. Villa at No. 1 Church Hill, built in 1842 as a residence for renowned Scottish churchman, Professor Thomas Chalmers, leader of the Disruption 1843. Dr. Chalmers died here on May 31st 1847.

91. East Morningside House, Colinton Road; the first villa built in Morningside c. 1726. House records bear first reference to Morning-side in the area, name perhaps derived from main door facing east — the "morning side of the sun". Jacobite troops visited the house while passing along to Holyrood 1745.

92. Susan Ferier who wrote her first novel "Marriage" (1818), published anonymously, in East Morningside House. More novels followed and she was hailed as "Scotland's Jane Austen", as well as being praised by close friend and visitor, Sir Walter Scott.

TIPPERLINN

93. Tipperlinn Road, behind Royal Edinburgh Hospital, commemoratively named. Original "High Street" of 17th century famed village of weavers, awarded a "By Royal Appointment".

94. A restoration of the Monarchy stone, dated 1660, whinch once stood in the pro-Royalist village of Tipperlinn. Now sited at entrance to former Tipperlinn House, the Royal Edinburgh Hospital's Young People's Unit.

95. The Edinburgh Bedlam, once at Bristo Port, in which the tragic death occurred in 1774 of 24-year old poetic genius, Robert Fergusson. This inspired his friend, Dr. Andrew Duncan, Sen., to found the first "Proper Asylum for the Insane" at Morningside, opened in 1813.

96. Dr. Andrew Duncan, Sen., with plan of his new asylum on his left. He was present at the laying of the foundation stone in 1809.

SKETCH OF THE ELEVATION SHEWING THE RANGE OF BUILDINGS WHICH FORM ONE SIDE OF THE SQUARE.

Scale of Feet

97. Architect's drawing by Robert Reid of the first "Proper Asylum" opened as the East House in Morningside in 1813, on the site between Maxwell Street and Morningside Park.

98. The first psychiatrists of the original Royal Edinburgh Hospital went to Paris to study the work of Dr Phillipe Pinel, famous pioneer in treatment of mental illness who released patients in the Bicêtre Hospital from their chains!
This memorial to him was opened beside McKinnon House, Royal Edinburgh Hospital in 1930, the first such tribute to Pinel anywhere.

99. Robert Fergusson, born 1750 and died 1774. Robert Burns acknowledged his own inspiration to him and arranged for the erection of his grave stone in Canongate Kirkyard.

100. Small chapel at the Royal Edinburgh Hospital, originally the "iron church" from St. Michael's, Slateford.

MORNINGSIDE VILLAGE

101. Panorama of Morningside and beyond.

102. Morningside Parish Church c. 1900.

103. The Bore Stone beside Morningside Parish Church. Reputedly the Scottish Standard was hoisted in a bore or hole in the stone during muster on the Burgh Muir prior to Scottish army's departure for Flodden. In fact, there is no authentic basis to this belief and it is probably just a march or boundary stone.

104. View from Churchhill c. 1900, from beside the Bore Stone. A stiff pull for the cable car!

105. At the north corner of Morningside Place, this old village stone "One Mile to Tollcross" still stands.

106. The original Manse of Morningside Parish Church was once "Mansewood" in Morningside Park. Eventually a new manse was purchased in Cluny Avenue.

107. Bank House, Albert Terrace off Churchhill, built c. 1790. The childhood home for some years of Cosmo Gordon Lang who became Archbishop of Canterbury, and mentioned in his biography.

108. Archbishop Cosmo Gordon Lang with Queen Mary.

109. Morningside's Old Schoolhouse opened in 1823. Closed c. 1900. Children attended from Swanston, Lothianburn and, of course, Morningside village itself.

10. Children at the Old Schoolhouse.

111. Children at the Old Schoolhouse.

112. Dick Wright's Smiddy in the old village, where the "Merlin" came to be built. Here, through the open door, passing school-house children watched the blacksmith producing "singed sheips heads". Became Blackford Press and joiner's premises.

113. The village blacksmith of c. 1900.

114. Morningside House (left) built c. 1790. The "big house" of the village. First owner, Lord Gardenstone, was an eccentric judge, succeeded by generations of the noted Deuchar family. The site today of Scotmid. This picture shows the joiner's shop and (right) Free Church School.

115. Denholm's Smiddy, the principal one of many is Morningside village. Here carters and farmers, coming in from the district and the south, brought their horses. The village grew up and around the smiddy c. 1780. Morningside Public Library was later built on its site.

116. Morningside Public Library, opened on the site of former Denholm's Smiddy 1904. It is one of the busiest branch libraries in Scotland.

117. The building of Springvalley Terrace and Gardens.

118. Just beyond the cottages was Morningside's first "picture" house, the Springvalley Cinema and, later, here was the Silver Slipper dance hall.

119. Row of cottages on the east side of Morningside road, facing today's Public Library on the boundary of Falcon Hall estate. Note cable car rails, gas street lamps and boys with golf clubs.

120. On the right (east side) of Morningside Road, may be seen two stout stone pillars of the gates to Falcon Hall. Removed c. 1910. A unique photograph. Today's location is between Nos. 193 and 195 Morningside Road.

121. The gates of drive-way to Falcon Hall c. 1910 were removed to the entrance to Zoo at Corstorphine where they remain.

122. Falcon Hall. Built c. 1815 by Alexander Falconar, retired wealthy Indian Civil Servant who worked in Madras, on the site on ar early house in Morningside Lodge. This was the other "big house" of the village. The Falconars, with 12 daughters, were local patrons of the schoolhouse and the parish church. The house was demolished around 1901.

123 & 125. After Falcon Hall's demolition, whilst the pillared frontage and interior staircase were retained and installed at Bartholomew's premises, the large figures of Nelson and Wellington disappeared. In fact, they were installed in the Italian garden at Lennel House in the Borders. In recent years, they were discovered in a sculptor's yard in London.

124. A popular brand in Morningside and possibly beyond.

126. The gates of Falcon Hall and at least two of the large stone falcons were transferred to the entrance of what became the Zoo.

127. After the demolition of Falcon Hall in 1901, Mr John Bartholomew, the mansion house's last owner, had its pillars and entrance carefully rebuilt and used as the frontage to his cartographer's premises in Duncan Street. Falcon Hall's fine interior staircase was also taken there.

128. Paradise cottages once stood between entrances to Canaan Lane and Jordan Lane in "village High Street". Yet another Biblical name!

129. The Volunteer's Rest, Morningside's earliest tavern at Canaan Lane and forerunner of the "Canny Man", built nearby in 1871. The Edinburgh Volunteers who practised shooting at Blackford Hill frequented the hostelry. Johnny Kerr, the first "Canny Man", so named for warning customers not to drink and drive - their horses! "Ca'canny, man!"

130. Sam Bough, RSA, noted landscape painter, resided in Jordan Lane (then Jordan Bank) 1867 until his death there the 1878. He painted two inn signs for the "Canny Man".

131. Morningside's first "St. Cuthberts Co-operative store", c. 1880, No. 241 Morningside Road. Several other premises followed before the present "Scotmid" supermarket.

132. Robert Main, one of Morningside's earliest family businesses, originated with a fishwife coming to Morningside daily. There have been a succession of premises. Gilmour Main is on the left of the picture .

133. One of many early laundries in Morningside. The pre-launderette era! After two supermarkets, the present Post Office was built on this site.

134. Early view (c. 1890) of shops between Nos. 243 and 251 Morningside Road. This shows the corner of Jordan Lane.

135. View during cable car era, introduced to Morningside in 1897. Early view, on right the Toll House area c. 1897.

136. Morningside's Toll House. It stood at Briggs o'Braid (actually the Jordan Burn) just within the ground of Braid Church beside Post Office. Tolls were abolished in 1883 and the Toll House was carefully dismantled and rebuilt as a gate lodge at Hermitage of Braid.

137. Before estate agents coined the phrase "shared common garden", the "back green" or common drying ground behind tenements formed a popular playground for many children. A happy group in a back green in Maxwell Street c. 1930. Itinerant photographers "cashed-in" on such scenes and sold the photographs.

138. The Kinderspiel or children's play was a common event for most Sunday Schools. This "gigantic cast" of all ages performed in "The Magic Key" in Braid Church, 1926.

139. The Sunday School picnic was an eagerly anticipated summer occasion. Trips were often by suburban railway. Tea urns and kettles were essential. Menu: pies and buns in paper bag! This scene was a Braid Church picnic, Craigmillar Castle, 1936.

140. Stone plaque commemorating Queen Victoria's Diamond Jubilee of 1897 built high up on the front wall of the tenement at Nos. 200—202 Morningside Road, probably at the time when it was built.

141. Pupils of South Morningside Primary School at Waverley Station in April 1980 about to have the first trip on the old Suburban Railway since its closure nearly twenty years before.

CANAAN

142. Morningside's large number of Biblical names of houses, streets and other locations always prompts curiosity. Origins probably lay in a gypsy colony in the early 16th century settled at the corner of Nile Grove and Braid Avenue. District is referred to in early records as "Littil Egypt". Canaan is the next name to appear. The others followed over the years.

143. Egypt Farm remained at the Nile Grove-Braid Avenue site until c. 1890. Last family there were the Begbie's with a family grave in Grange cemetery.

144. Canaan Lane: ancient and modern. The Goshen district on right. Falcon Court opposite.

145. Goshen Bank House a short distance along on south side of Canaan Lane. Henry Kingsley resided here in 1869. In 1874, Reginald Johnston was born here. He attended nearby Falcon Hall private school. He was to become tutor to the last (boy) Emperor of China. Johnston featured in the film "The Last Emperor".

146. Reginald Johnston in China. Peter O'Toole played the part of Johnston in the film. Johnston died in Edinburgh in 1938.

147. Canaan Lodge, built in 1907 on site of earlier villa destroyed by fire. The earlier house was the residence of Professor James Gregory, famous for his powder, for long a regular Saturday night children's tonic for the stomach.

148. Professor James Gregory of Canaan Lodge.

149. The original recipe for Gregory's Powder. The rhubarb required was grown by Dr Alexander Dick of Prestonfield House, who introduced it to Britain, and the magnesia was manufactured by Dr Thomas Steel in his Morningside factory, commemorated in the name Steel's Place.

150. Canaan Lodge in more elegant days.

151. On the boundary wall of Canaan Lodge in Canaan Lane, two stones indicate a passage underground here: "5" and "7" pipes bringing Edinburgh's first piped water supply first from Comiston (1681) and later Swanston (1761). The pipes eventually went underground to Castlehill Reservoir.

152. Woodburn House, another classical villa of the Canaan district. Built in 1812 cost — £300! Once the home of George Ross, advocate, who for long managed Morningside's Old Schoolhouse single handed. Later a Royal Infirmary nurses' home.

154. Wedding photograph of Joseph Lister and Agnes Syme, April 1856.

153. Millbank Villa, once in what are now the grounds of the Astley Ainslie Hospital. Purchased by James Syme, the famous Edinburgh surgeon, in 1842. Here, in the drawing room, Syme's daughter Agnes married the even more famous Joseph Lister in 1856. House demolished c. 1931.

155. Today's hospital Commemorative Plaque.

THIS PAVILION
WAS ERECTED ON THE SITE OF MILLBANK.
THE RESIDENCE OF
JAMES SYME
PROFESSOR OF CLINICAL SURGERY (1833-1869)
IN THE DRAWING-ROOM AT MILLBANK
JOSEPH LISTER
WAS MARRIED TO SYME'S DAUGHTER, AGNES
ON APRIL 24TH 1856

156. Canaan Park villa, where the Astley Ainslie Hospital was first established in 1923. It has been also a private school for girls. The House remains as administrative offices.

157. Canaan Park soon after it became the original experimental unit of the Astley Ainslie Hospital. Its balcony was enlarged. Here patients were kept outside during the day and even during the night to obtain the maximum sunshine and fresh air, then an important part of the hospital's convalescent treatment.

158. Preparations by the "sand baggers" when the Astley Ainslie Hospital (founded 1923) became a Military Hospital during World War II.

159. St. Peter's Church, Falcon Avenue, built by Sir Robert Lorimer in 1907. Largely financed by the gift of André Raffalovitch of nearby Whitehouse Terrace. Canon Gray, first parish priest, scholar and poet was an early friend of Oscar Wilde.

160. Eden Lane, a truly "old world" part of the "Land of Canaan".

161. Dusk in Eden Lane.

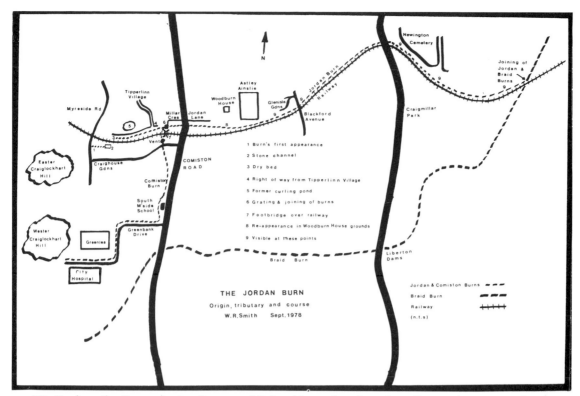

THE JORDAN BURN

Origin, tributary and course

W.R.Smith   Sept.1978

1 Burn's first appearance
2 Stone channel
3 Dry bed
4 Right of way from Tipperlinn Village
5 Former curling pond
6 Grating & joining of burns
7 Footbridge over railway
8 Re-appearance in Woodburn House grounds
9 Visible at these points

Jordan & Comiston Burns
Braid Burn
Railway
(n.t.s)

162. For long the Pow or Jordan Burn was Edinburgh's southern boundary, flowing from Myreside by Blackford, Mayfield and Newington on to the sea at Portobello. This plan shows its course.

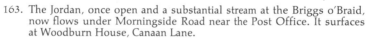

163. The Jordan, once open and a substantial stream at the Briggs o'Braid, now flows under Morningside Road near the Post Office. It surfaces at Woodburn House, Canaan Lane.

164. During the construction of the Post Office telephone building at the end of Maxwell Street, considerable water at this junction of the Jordan and Comiston burns required months of pumping operations.

165. Water can be a powerful force. Here at Morningside Road, where the Jordan Burn flows underground, nearby foundations were undermined and part of the tenement had to be taken down.

166. The ancient Jordan — referred to in records of 1497 — could still cause underground damage to these tenements.

MORNINGSIDE STATION, EDINBURGH.

167. Morningside Station area c. 1912. The telegram boys stand ready to run with urgent messages to the "big houses" of the Cluny area. The clock was installed in 1910. The "cabbies" wait on the right.

168. Morningside Station c. 1900. Note the horse-drawn tram on the left. Two horses are being rested before their turn to climb up Churchill again. Once frequent railway transport was available the suburb of Morningside mushroomed almost overnight.

169. The construction of part of Maxwell Street and the adjoining section of Morningside Road, originally named Watt Terrace, completed in 1877. Braid Church was yet to be built.

170. Morningside Road Station was opened on the Edinburgh Suburban and South Side Junction Railway during its establishment in 1884. Trains ran every 10 minutes during the peak hours. The many commuters provided substantial revenue.

171. The Suburban Railway in its heyday. Boys watch from the Morningside Station footbridge. The trains were crowded when Hearts were playing at home. Gorgie Station was reached in minutes.

172. The laying of the foundation stone of Braid Church, October 1886. The church was completed nine months later! This was architect, Sir George Washington Browne's first public building. It had quite a unique interior auditorium design.

173. St Matthew's Church, Cluny Gardens, foundation was laid in June 1888. A large church of fine cathedral-like design by Hippolyte Blanc, building took two years. The architect is second from right with hand on stone.

174. The construction of the then proposed Belhaven Hotel in c. 1884 at the corner of Braid Road and Comiston Road. Funds ran out and plans were abandoned. Flats were built instead.

175. The junction of Braid Road, the old straight Roman road from the South, and the later Comiston Road.

176. Popular grocer and wine merchant at corner of Comiston Road and Craiglea Drive.

177. Comiston Road beyond Morningside Station became famous for family businesses. In Torrance's first floor tea-rooms many Morningside developments were first discussed.

178. St Matthew's Church, Cluny Gardens. Beyond is the spire of the original South Morningside Church, united with St. Matthew's in 1974 to form Cluny Parish Church.

BLACK FORD

179. Blackford House was beside one-time Blackford Hill Station. Painting by an itinerant artist. Miss Menie Trotter who lived here c. 1800 reputedly "bathed daily in the Jordan" flowing past. She rests with a friend, a servant works!

180. Blackford farmhouse: now modern flats. Note the little stone bridge over the Jordan Burn.

181. Blackford Hill Station. A busy place with sheep-pens, the sheep being kept on nearby Blackford Hill and transported by rail. Blackford House in the centre of picture.

182. In 1984, to celebrate the centenary of Blackford Hill's acquisition, a seat to commemorate Lord Provost George Harrison was placed on Blackford's summit, by his nonogenarian grandson, Sandy, and family.

183. Blackford Quarry, opened 1826, taking over from destructive quarrying at Salisbury Crags. Closed 1952.

184. The Agassiz Rock, in Blackford Glen, near the disused Quarry. Here the famous Swiss geologist, Louis Agassiz, in 1840, identified evidence to proclaim: "This is the work of the ice", or ancient glacier action.

85. The Harrison Arch in Observatory Road, off Blackford Hill, honours Sir George Harrison for his considerable public service in Edinburgh and as a Member of Parliament.

186. Blackford Pond, one of Edinburgh's most pleasant "lochs". Countless tons of breadcrumbs have fed innumerable ducks.

187. "The Bonspiel". Once, and for long, a happy winter scene on Blackford Pond. Families from all around and youngsters took to the ice. Morningside shops displayed notices: "Pond bearing today".

188. A view from Blackford Hill over Mortonhall Road and beyond. Blackford farmhouse can be seen on right.

THE BRAIDS & THE HERMITAGE

189. Workmen re-set the two "hanging stones" in Braid Road where previously only one was visible. These stones supported gallows on which two men were hanged at this spot on January 25th 1815 for a robbery nearby.

190. On the right, the Braidburn Dairy (c. 1900) opposite the entrance to the Hermitage of Braid. The scene of the notorious Braid Road robbery.

191. The gate lodge at the entrance to Hermitage of Braid was originally Morningside's toll house beside the Jordan Burn. Erected here c. 1883. On the side lintel is number "269", the original Morningside Road street number.

192. The dovecot near Hermitage of Braid mansion house in reputedly very ancient, dating back to Braid Castle, perhaps as long ago as the 12th century. It had 1,965 pigeon holes.

193. Mansion of Hermitage of Braid built in 1785 by Charles Goron of Cluny. His Aberdeenshire estate and other lands were commemorated by district streets names such as Corrennie and Midmar. After many owners and tenants, now a most attractive Countryside Information Centre.

194. Charles Gordon of Cluny's wife and family in Hermitage of Braid. Early house in the background. From a painting in oils by Alexander Nasmyth, c. 1790.

195. The curling pond which became Morton-Hall Tennis Courts in Braid Road, beside Braid Burn.

196. Braid Farm (or Upper or Nether Braid) from Braid Hills. The early farmhouse remains. In it, Robert Burn's "Fair Burnet" died of tuberculosis in June 1790.

197. Edinburgh Corporation opened Braid Hills public golf course in 1889. The "Evening Dispatch" campaigned for the acquisition of the Braids. The annual "Dispatch Trophy" golf tournament commemorates the newspapers's efforts.

198. Cable car, from Pilrig to Morningside Station. It eventually increased its run to the Braid terminus.

199. Buckstane farmhouse, Braid Road, and on the left of gate stands the Buckstane. It is an ancient stone, once on other side of road, where Scottish kings unchained their hounds when they arrived to hunt on the Pentland Hills.

200. Two famous golfers of c. 1900. Harry Vardon (British Open Championship five times) and James Braid (also frequent Open champion). Braid advised on layout of the Braid Hills course.

201. A frequently waterlogged area of the Braid Hills provided a good skating rink in winter.

202. The Buckstane was moved to its present site through efforts of Mr James S. Bennet who resided in the farmhouse. At the installation ceremony in 1964, Mr Bennet holds the Scottish flag. Sir John Clerk of Penecuik with the hunting horn, — still obliged to give three blasts if the monarch came here to hunt!

203. An early fishwife from Fisherrow who came out to Morningside, mainly on foot with her heavy creel, then went round the "big houses".

204. Fishwife today, Mrs Betty Millar, the last of the colourful ladies to journey to Morningside (actually to Buckstane, on certain days) opening her kerb-side shop. Now — by van — the "creel on wheels" and the skirt not so lengthy!

FAIRMILEHEAD

Fairmilehead, Edinburgh.

205. Fairmilehead. "A place where four roads meet", wrote Stevenson, "and the air comes brisk and sweetly off the hills". Here in Robert Louis Stevenson's day was a Post Office and a toll house.

206. The man who pioneered the way for the establishment of an orthopaedic hospital for children was the Reverend Dr T. Ratcliffe Barnett, minister of Greenbank Church and a prolific author on the Highlands, the Borders and much else.

207. Mortonhall House, Frogston Road East, built 1769. Architect was John Baxter. One of seats of the Trotters of Morton-hall and Charterhall, Berwickshire. House now converted into flats.

208. The Princess Margaret Rose Hospital at Fairmilehead, opened in 1933, was originally for crippled children. Regularly army band performers came out to the hospital to the delight of the young patients.

209. Bowbridge farmhouse on Biggar Road, below Fairmilehead. Here the gauger came to inspect whisky stocks (there was an illicit still) in Stevenson's "Edinburgh Picturesque Notes". Farmhouse demolished to make way for bypass road nearby.

210. Morton House, Winton, off Frogston Road West: early 18th century, enlarged in early 19th century, it has many interesting architectural features. It was built as dower house for the Trotter family of nearby Mortonhall House.

211. The Belvedere of Morton House. Probably early 18th century. A fine view to the Pentland Hills.

PLEWLANDS & CRAIGHOUSE

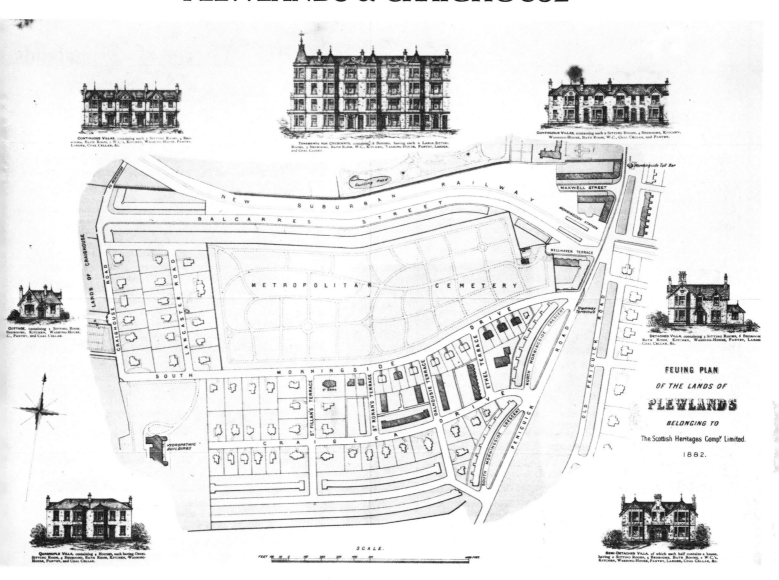

CONTINUOUS VILLAS, containing each 2 Sitting Room, 3 Bedrooms, Bath Room, 1 W.C.'s, Kitchen, Washing-House, Pantry, Larder, Coal Cellar, &c.

TENEMENTS FOR CRESCENTS, containing 8 Houses, having each 1 Large Sitting Room, 3 Bedrooms, Bath Room, W.C., Kitchen, Washing-House, Pantry, Larder, and Coal Closet.

CONTINUOUS VILLAS, containing each 2 Sitting Rooms, 4 Bedrooms, Kitchen, Washing-House, Bath Room, W.C., Coal Cellar, and Pantry.

COTTAGE, containing 1 Sitting Room, Bedrooms, Kitchen, Washing-House, &c., Pantry, and Coal Cellar.

DETACHED VILLA, containing 3 Sitting Rooms, 6 Bedroom, Bath Room, Kitchen, Washing-House, Pantry, Larder, Coal Cellar, &c.

FEUING PLAN

OF THE LANDS OF

PLEWLANDS

BELONGING TO

The Scottish Heritages Compy. Limited.

1882.

QUADRUPLE VILLA, containing 4 Houses, each having Oriel, Sitting Room, 4 Bedrooms, Bath Room, Kitchen, Washing-House, Pantry, and Coal Cellar.

SEMI-DETACHED VILLA, of which each half contains a house, having 2 Sitting Rooms, 3 Bedrooms, Bath Room, 2 W.C.'s, Kitchen, Washing-House, Pantry, Larder, Coal Cellar, &c.

SCALE.

3. World-famous golfer Tommy Armour first played in 9-hole course at end of Balcarres Street then on Braids. Became professional tutor to American presidents.

4. There are very many graves of interest in Morningside cemetery. Here rests Robert Louis Stevenson's beloved childhood nurse "Cummy" — Alison Cunningham — who died (in Morningside) July 21st, 1913.

215. Dr Douglas Strachan, a stained glass artist of world renown had his studio through a pend in Balcarres Street. In 1925, he was visited there by Queen Mary.

216. Morningside Hydropathic shown on 1882 Plewlands feuing plan, on what is now north west open space in Morningside Grove. Hydro apparently soon failed and became the very select Morningside College later in 1882. The masters were Oxford and Cambridge dons.

217. Invitation to the opening of Morningside College.

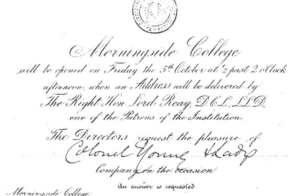

Morningside College

will be opened on Friday the 5th October at ½ past 2 o'Clock afternoon, when an Address will be delivered by

The Right Hon Lord Reay, D.C.L, LL.D, one of the Patrons of the Institution.

The Directors request the pleasure of Colonel Young & Lady Company on the occasion

An answer is requested.

Morningside College,
24th September 1883.

This Card to be presented at the Door.

218. A water colour painting of early Plewlands district, perhaps c. 1880, viewed from the Hydro. Substantial buildings and attractive farmhouse of important Plewlands farm are seen.

219. In 1889, Morningside College moved to "Rockcliffe", James Gowan's vacated house in Napier Road (and finally Falcon Hall). College premises became Plewlands House and here the patients of the Royal Hospital for Children came temporarily from original hospital near Lauriston Lane. The fine Sciennes Hospital was opened in 1895.

220. The avenue shown here led straight to Old Craig. After the Asylum opened, anothers gate was built to the south and the drive-way curved up to the house, as today.

221. The completed Craighouse Asylum, opened in 1894. The architect was Sydney Mitchell. The cost was £150,000 — considered a large sum at that time. The building had every possible facility to make wealthy patients' stay amenable.

222. Laying of foundation stone at Craighouse, July 1890. Hospital opened 1894. Dr Thomas Coulston, the Medical Superintendant, was the prime mover in acquiring the site on Craighouse Hill.

223. Dr Thomas Coulston, Physician Superintendant of the Royal Edinburgh Asylum (now Hospital) 1873—1908. An Orcadian, Dr Coulston, a scholar and dynamic personality, represented a new era in treatment of mental illness. Note dates of buildings.

West House 1840

TARY DINNER
NTATION TO
ON, M.D., F.R.C.P.E., LLD
the Royal Edinburgh Asylum
and present Medical
EDINBURGH
une 1908.

224. The Grand Hall, Craighouse. Used for banquets, musical recitals (note Minstrel's Gallery at back). Also used for cinema shows.

225. The building of Craighouse progresses. A private hospital, many patients were very wealthy, often from titled families. Suites of rooms were available and servants could be engaged.

226. The Grand Hall at Craighouse, apart from accommodating banquets and musical recitals, had cinema shows. A very old type of arc-lamp projector was recently discovered on the roof outside the Grand Hall windows.

227. The projector, kept in a wooden hut on the roof, was wheeled on rails to the Grand Hall windows. The projector lens was introduced through a removable glass pane.

CRAIGLOCKHART

228. Craiglockhart Hydropathic as originally opened under the north side of West Craiglockhart Hill in 1880. The Hydro was for a period much in demand.

229. The prospectus of Craiglockhart Hydropathic. Every attention was given by doctors, nurses and house maids.

Prayers in Lounge every morning after Breakfast, and on Sundays at 9 P.M.

MEALS.—Breakfast (8 A.M. for those requiring it) at - - - - - 9 A.M.
Luncheon at - - - - - - - - 1.30 P.M.
Afternoon Tea - - - - - - - - 4 P.M.
Dinner - - - - - - - - 7 P.M.
Tea and Coffee - - - - - - - - 8 P.M.
Dinner at 8 P.M. on Sundays.
Serving Meals in Parlour or Bedroom 6d. extra each meal per visitor. Visitors may entertain their friends at the following rates:—Breakfast, 2.6; Luncheon, 2—; Dinner, 3.6; Plain Tea, 1/-. Afternoon Tea is served from 4 to 4.30, after which time it is charged extra.
The Warning Bell is rung at 8 A.M., and also 15 minutes before each meal. The Gong is sounded at the hours of meals.

BATHS.—In the Basement—Turkish, Russian, and Swimming Baths are open for Gentlemen from 6.30 to 8 A.M. and from 3 to 5.30 P.M. daily, except Tuesdays; for Ladies from 10 a.m. to 1 p.m. daily, except Tuesdays. On Tuesdays for Gentlemen from 6.30 to 8 a.m., and 10 a.m. to 1 p.m.; for Ladies, 3 to 5.30 p.m. Plunge, Spray, etc., Baths, from 6.30 to 8 a.m., 10 a.m. to 1 p.m., and 3 to 5.30 p.m., for both Ladies and Gentlemen.
A charge is made for Baths in Bedrooms and in Bathrooms in Corridors, and for Medicated Baths. Swimming Lessons, 7/6 per dozen. Massage Treatment, 2.6 per visit.

LIGHTS AND ATTENDANCE.—Gas must be extinguished in Bedrooms during the night. Night Lights can be obtained at the Office if required. Lights in the Public Rooms are extinguished at 10.30 p.m.; in the Smoking and Billiard Rooms at 11 p.m. No attendance to be expected from servants after 10 P.M.

WASHING.—Lists of Clothes sent to the Laundry must be made on the Duplicate forms provided, and all articles must be marked, otherwise the Management will not be responsible.

FARES TO STATIONS.—Waverley, 4/-; Princes Street, 3/-; Haymarket, 2.6; Merchiston, 2/-.

ACCOUNTS are rendered weekly from the day of arrival. Cheques cannot be taken in payment unless presented three days before departure.

NOTICE OF DEPARTURE to be given at least one day previous, and in July, August, and September three days when possible.

VALUABLES.—The Management will not be responsible for any Valuables lost in the Establishment, unless they are left at the Office accompanied with a written memorandum.

Motors are kept and parties will be arranged. Full particulars given at the Office.

AFTERNOON VISITS can be made to Forth Bridge, Roslin, Craigmillar, Hawthornden, Dalkeith, Palace, Hopetoun, Dalmeny, Linlithgow, and day excursions to Abbotsford, Peebles, Melrose, Dryburgh, The Trossachs, and to Forth and Clyde for Marine Trips. Swanston Cottage, the birthplace of R. L. Stevenson, is within walking distance.

FEATURES.—Splendid Croquet Lawns, the largest and finest in Scotland. The Scottish Championship Meeting is held here annually, also numerous Competitions and Tournaments. Excellent Golfing in the neighbourhood. Tennis Courts. Bowling Greens.

PRINCIPAL CHURCHES IN EDINBURGH:—
Established Church of Scotland.—St Giles, High Street; St Cuthbert's, Lothian Road; St George's, Charlotte Square.
United Free Church of Scotland.—St George's, Shandwick Place; Barclay, Bruntsfield Links; St Mary's, Broughton Street; Palmerston Place Church; Morningside Church.
Episcopalian.—St Marys Cathedral, Palmerston Place; St John's, West End of Princes Street; St Pauls, York Place.
Roman Catholic.—St Marys (Pro-Cathedral), Broughton Street.

PLACES OF INTEREST IN EDINBURGH:—
The Castle; University, South Bridge; United Free Church College, The Mound; Surgeons Hall, Nicolson Street; National Gallery, Princes Street; Scottish National Portrait Gallery, Queen Street; John Knox's House, High Street; Greyfriar's Churchyard (Martyr's Monument); Antiquarian Museum, Queen Street; Royal Scottish Museum...

230. This is a unique souvenir of the Hydropathic: a letter from the noted Morningside water-colour painter Miss Hannah Preston Macgoun whose father was minister of Morningside Parish Church. She illustrated Dr John Brown's classic: "Rab and His Friends".

TELEPHONE
CENTRAL No. 5045.

TELEGRAPHIC ADDRESS
"HYDROPATHIC, SLATEFORD"

POSTAL ADDRESS EDINBURGH HYDROPATHIC COY. LD.
SLATEFORD,
MIDLOTHIAN.

15th June 1912

Dear Mr Page
When I saw how appreciative you were of the little books this morning, I wished I had brought you the whole set of 5.—
I send the other 3 now, for your kind acceptance, & hope you may have as much pleasure in receiving them as I have in sending them to you.—
Yrs sincerely
H. J. Preston Macgoun

231. During World War I, Craiglockhart Hydro became a military hospital for officers from the front suffering from shell shock or other nervous disorders. Here is Siegfried Sassoon (left).

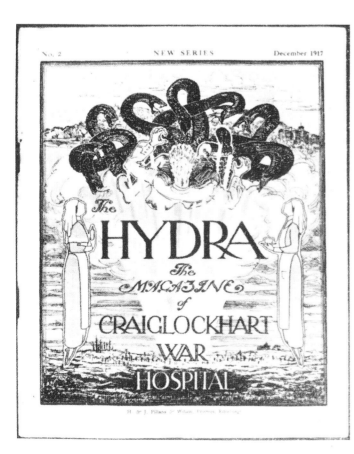

232. Wilfred Owen came to Craiglockhart Hospital in June 1917 having been shell-shocked in the battle of the Somme. One of his contributions to the hospital magazine was the well-known poem "Anthem for Doomed Youth". He taught English literature at Tynecastle School and took pupils on visits to Stevenson's former home at Swanston Cottage. After discharge at the end of August 1918 he returned to the front where he was killed.

233. During their stay in the hospital, Sassoon wrote much poetry, played golf at Mortonhall and frequented Princes Street clubs, and Owen taught English. Together they edited "The Hydra" the hospital magazine, which first published some of their best poetry.

GREENBANK

234. The City Poorhouse, Glenlockhart Road, under wester Craiglockhart Hill, facing the City Hospital. Conditions were rigorous. Eventually became Glenlockhart Old People's Home, then Greenlea. Closed 1987 but frontage is to be preserved.

235. In May 1870, Craiglockhart Poorhouse was opened, succeeding the city's early Charity Workhouse at Forrest Road. A special driveway was opened from Comiston Road. This gate lodge remained until demolition in 1988.

236. For long, infectious diseases cases in Edinburgh were isolated in hospitals at the Canongate and the former vacated surgical wing of old Royal Infirmary, Infirmary Street. After long campaign and controversy, Colinton Fever Hospital opened in 1903: today's City Hospital. Edward VII performs opening ceremony of the new fever hospital, May 13th 1903, in presence of Lord Provost James Steel and many dignitaries (above and below).

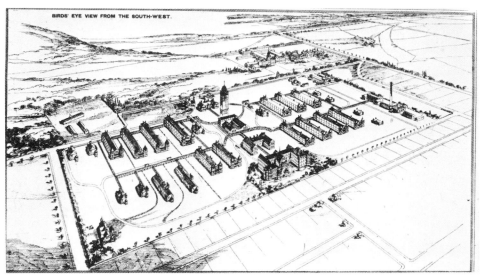

237. The plan of the proposed City Hospital at Colinton Mains. Architect, Robert Morhan. Costing £350,000, the hospital was unsurpassed in Britain. Note symmetry of Florence Nightingale-type, north-south wards.

240. Daily newspaper "Bulletin". On account of the distance from city centre before the prevelance of cars and telephones, and since infectious patients could not be visited, the City Hospital published a daily "Bulletin" in Edinburgh's "Evening Dispatch" and "Evening News", giving news of patients' progress.

EDINBURGH CITY HOSPITAL.

TO-DAY'S BULLETIN.

Seriously ill; no immediate danger: 6, 39, 44 61, 66, 73, 74, 286, 591, 630, 697, 711, 726, 750, 769, 788, 860, 895, 908, 947, 962, 987, 990.

Ill; making satisfactory progress meantime: 1, 4, 5, 9, 10, 15, 17, 20, 21, 22, 24, 27, 28, 30, 31, 32, 33, 34, 35, 36, 37, 38, 40, 41, 42, 43, 45, 46, 47, 49, 50, 51, 52, 53, 54, 55, 56, 57, 58, 59, 60, 62, 64, 65, 67, 68, 69, 70, 71, 72, 306, 407, 478, 615, 640, 670, 742, 763, 778, 802, 809, 816, 828, 840, 861, 863, 867, 882, 891, 893, 898, 899, 901, 902, 907, 913, 918, 919, 921, 922, 926, 930, 937, 939, 947, 950, 952, 953, 954, 955, 956, 957, 961, 963, 968, 969, 971, 972, 973, 974, 975, 977, 98, 981, 982, 985, 986, 988, 989, 991, 992, 993, 994, 995, 997, 999.

It may be concluded that all patients whose numbers are not referred to in this bulletin are making satisfactory progress.

241. The entrance to the attractive Braidburn Valley park, opened in 1937. The stout stone gate pillars were once at the entrance to Comiston House at Camus Avenue and transferred here.

242. The Braidburn Valley open air theatre, with natural tiered auditorium, resembling a crown, completed by John T. Jeffrey, then City Gardener, for the Coronation of George VI and Queen Elizabeth. Before World War II, many performances were held but there have been few since.

238. *Opposite:* Dr Henry Littlejohn, Edinburgh's first Medical Officer of Health, served 1862—1908. Made vast contribution towards advancing health of the city. Pioneered the new City Fever Hospital.

239. *Opposite:* The surrounding ground is crowded and the Horse Guards stand to attention as Edward VII and Queen Alexandra enter new hospital's gates. The city was bedecked with grandstands to watch the Royal procession to Greenbank.

Old Cottage, Greenbank, Morningside
"within a mile o' Edinburgh toun".

243. Old thatched cottage which stood beside the path high up on west side of the Braid Burn Valley. This path, still there, entered by Fly Walk off Greenbank Crescent, was taken by R. L. Stevenson walking out to Swanston Cottage.

244. Greenbank farmhouse stood to the north side of Greenbank Crescent. An important farm of considerable acreage and varied crops. Artists and writers often lived at Greenbank Farm.

COMISTON

245. South Morningside Primary School in Comiston Road was opened in 1892. Andrew Carnegie attended the opening ceremony. Children assembled on a special occasion c. 1900.

246. A school class at South Morningside School c. 1900.

247. With the introduction of Edinburgh's first piped water supply, brought from the many springs at Comiston, the water ran into a tank into this collecting house, above Oxgangs Avenue. From here it travelled underground to Castlehill.

248. In 1945, new housing developments around Comiston created a danger of contamination and — Edinburgh by then having greatly increased supplies — the original Comiston supply was released into the Braid Burn, beside the bridge at Oxgangs Avenue.

249. The early Comiston springs were given animal's names: Hare, the Tod (or fox), the Swan and Peewit. A lead fig of these animals sat at the exit of each pipe into the colle ing tank. Figures now in Huntly House Museum.

250. Castlehill Reservoir beside the Castle Esplanade. Comiston, and later Swanston springs water piped here under districts of Cluny, Canaan, Marchmont, the Meadows and Grassmarket, then steeply up to Castlehill.

251. Comiston House, a fine classical villa reached by Camus Avenue, was built by Lord Provost James Forrest in 1815. Manor House of Comiston Estate. Became a hotel and now contains flats.

252. The gateway to Comiston House when standing at Camus Avenue. Rebuilt as entrance to Hermitage of Braid.

EDINBURGH. HARVEST-TIME AT COMISTON

253. At Comiston farm. The Pentland Hills form the back-cloth.

254. Ruins of an ancient castle near Comiston House.

255. The ancient Caiystane, Camus Stane, Kel or Cat Stane — various names — when isolated in a field just beyond Comiston. Morningside man, Mr W. E. Evans, photographed it.

256. The Caiy Stane now standing in Caiystane View near Fairmilehead.

257. An early scene at the Braid Burn.

258. A winter panorama over Firhill, Comiston and Oxgangs area, taken from high flats at Firhill. Comiston House is in the woods, top left. The 1766 planted "T" wood stands out clearly.

259. Oxgangs farm once stood beside police station at Oxgangs Road North. Robert Louis Stevenson, living at Swanston, knew the farmer and often here reputedly wrote poetry under an old cedar tree still be seen.

260. At Oxgangs farm Robert Louis Stevenson once carved his name on a wooden door and beneath wrote "5'83/4" — stocking soles". Is now in a little Stevenson museum in Oxgangs Primary School.

261. Breeders of pointer horses once used to meet at Hunters Tryst.

262. Hunters Tryst Inn, Oxgangs Road North. Some such tryst reputedly there in early centuries for hunters on Pentland Hills. First shown on a map of 1747, the Inn's heyday was in the early 19th century. Here met the Six Foot Athletic Club and it features in Stevenson's "St. Ives".

263. Hunters Tryst inn closed c. 1862: it became the dairy farm and piggery of Rogers family. In 1970's opened as a well-appointed restaurant. Old Milestone here was stopping place for London stagecoach.

SWANSTON

264. "This, with the hamlet lying behind unseen, is Swanston..." wrote Stevenson looking down from top of Swanston Road. Swanston Cottage largely hidden in trees on the right of the farm building and thus often missed by visitors. Farmhouse c. 1700 is amidst trees middle left.

265. "The municipal pleasure house..." again Stevenson's words for the original Swanston Cottage built as rendezvous for City bailies and officials when Swanston springs water supply was first opened in 1761.

266. Originally, small, almost primitive, Swanston Cottage was gradually altered and enlarged over the years. Bow windows were installed by Stevenson's parents 1867. He resided here with them 1867—1880. His bedroom centre on upper floor.

267. The cottages of Swanston village (early 18th century) restored c. 1960, have a romantic, "chocolate box" appearance. In fact, in early days cottages were mostly two-roomed, with an earthen floor, adjacent midden and no proper bedrooms, yet farm workers families were often large.

268. The Swanston hay-makers. The steep, 1568-feet high scar-faced Caerketton rises above them. Stevenson saw the figures of "the 7 sisters" in Caerketton's scree-covered, rocky face.

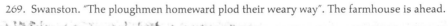

269. Swanston. "The ploughmen homeward plod their weary way". The farmhouse is ahead.

270. Spring in Swanston village. The gable end of John Todd's cottage in centre. The two-storey White House was the village school.

271. Swanston children exchange the news of the day! The schoolhouse is on the right.

272. Swanston village in winter. On the left of picture, the gable end of John Todd, the Swanston's shepherd's cottage. The two-storey house on right was for long the village school. Called the Whitehouse, it is now a fine residential villa.

273. A group of villagers. John Todd's wife is second from the left in second row with her small boy.

274. Lord Charles Guthrie, a judge and once close friend of
Stevenson, subsequently acquired Swanston Cottage.
He often brought Cummy out there as his guest. Here
they are in the Quarry Garden.

275. While she was living at Balcarres Street, notable people
often wished to meet Cummy and talk of Stevenson.
Lord Guthrie would arrange for such meetings at Swanston Cottage. Here Cummy is at the door with the
Duchess of Sutherland.

276. After Stevenson finally left Edinburgh, "Cummy" his
beloved childhood nurse remained at Swanston with
her brother, a water worker, till 1893, then moved to
No. 23 Balcarres Street in Morningside. She is seen
there, with Louis' picture before her.

277. Robert Young, the Swanston Cottage gardener preferred vegetables to flowers and grew cabbages in the rose beds!

278. A Swanston cottager and her feathered friend.

279. The past comes to life. In 1978, readings from Stevenson's work were given to audiences at Swanston Cottage by Scottish actor, John Sheddon. The event was arranged by the Scottish Tourist Board.

280. John Todd the Swanston shepherd. He became a close friend of young Stevenson when he lived at Swanston Cottage. They walked the hills together, Stevenson being deeply impressed and influenced by Todd's adventurous tales and, wrote RLS, "the richest dialect of Scotch I ever heard".